I0407704

CONCISE ILLUSTRATIONS OF

Personality

CHANGE

MATTHEW JAMES DICKEN

CONCISE ILLUSTRATIONS OF PERSONALITY CHANGE

FOR MY PARENTS

for raising me to believe that anything was possible

with a bit of hard work and determination.

Table of Contents

Introduction

CHANGING PERSONALITY

Over the course of a person's life they experience many changes and developments. Hand in hand with this comes changes within a person's psyche which manifests itself as changes in personality characteristics, cognitive function and behavioural action. These personality changes can happen gradually or can happen as sudden life events. Similarly, we might note that some personality changes produce long term effects whilst others do not last and therefore only produce short term effects (Carstensen et al., 2010. p.367). Some personality changes can be seen as healthy and producing desirable personality traits and behavioural characteristics (Lall & Sharma, 2012, p.245). Whilst other changes in personality are seen as demonstrative of a decline in general happiness, degenerative cognitive functionality and producing undesirable personality characteristics, behaviour and traits (Fleminger, 2010, p.205).

During this text, we will attempt to establish that personality change is not only possible but that it happens to each person on every day of their lives. We will attempt to scope out the reasons behind personality changes. We must note here that this text will not give full and exhaustive list of the reasons behind personality change as it is not humanly possible to be able to cover every reason for the conscious and, as Freud would note, the unconscious mind's personality changes. Rather, this text will attempt to categorise a series of the most significant reasons for personality change which will then help us to understand how human personality is not static and constantly develops.

In order to do this successfully and effectively, we will look at an illustration of each type of change derived from literature, non-fiction memoirs, historical, sacred and philosophical texts. The illustrations given will help us to ground theory in a more concrete and tangible manner. With exposition, these illustrations will help us to understand the parameters of personality change and lead us to analytical examination of current research literature and studies. The illustrations will also help us to establish that the ideas behind personality change are not new but that they are rooted in the very fabric of our culture, philosophy and values.

A note must be made at this point to state that not all psychologists and psychiatrists believe that an individual's personality has a certain plasticity. Some psychologists have been keen to stress the 'stable' nature of personality rather than its 'dynamic' nature (Tickle, 2001, pp.242-243). For instance, some have stated that, after the age of approximately thirty years old, personality almost ceases to have the ability to change. William James, in the Nineteenth Century, describes it as 'set in plaster and will never soften again' (James, 1890, p.124). However, Haslam et al. (2007) note that there is substantial evidence to show that personality shows 'rank-order stability' but there is 'ample evidence that the mean levels of many traits change across the life-course'.

We need not look further than our own lives to be able to show that we, ourselves, have developed and, as we recognise from change theory, are constantly going through the process of change. If we take this realisation, it would be naïve of us to believe that our personalities are immune to external changes, our own physical changes and events in our lives. We might summarise by saying that we, as human beings, are not the same person we were five years ago and neither will we be the same person we are today in another five years. This work will seek to demonstrate that a person might retain some enduring personality characteristics but might relinquish others and adopt new characteristics thus changing their personality slightly or even to an almost unrecognisable state.

The categories of personality change, outlined on the next pages by the author, lay out nine sets of reasons for personality changes, however, they at times overlap and, it is our belief, that in reality a simple diagnosis of one simple cause of personality change would be a false construct.

In the soup of the mind, a person can possess multiple reasons behind their personality changes. In short, the human mind is extremely complex and personality changes are equally as complex, however, this book will attempt to analyse and breakdown the complex tapestry of the mind's changes into a series of individual threads that are underlying and that subsequently form a foundation for personality change. However, before we do just that, we need to examine what we mean by the term 'personality'.

Chapter One

DEFINING PERSONALITY

Popular culture and everyday parlance use the term 'personality' very freely. People use it as a way of defining characteristics of a person: "She has a strong personality". People use it to differentiate between themselves and others: "He has a unique personality." When we describe a person, we can describe their looks and visible features, but then we can also describe their character and their non-visible characteristics. It is that non-visible, almost non-tangible, set of characteristics that we label as 'personality'.

In essence, personality is a common term, that we use in our general day-to-day language to talk about 'who we are'. It is about personal identity and about identification with others. However, just as scientists have discovered that the universe is ever expanding, when we try to pin down the meaning of 'personality' and attempt to form a definition, it is a topic which is ever expanding to encompass everything that makes a person who they are, who they were and who they want to become.

Tickle, Heatherton & Wittenberg (2001, pp.243-258) describe personality as a set of dimensions to which we can attribute trait adjectives e.g. 'friendly, independent, conscientious, caring, arrogant'. However, with this idea that personality inhabits the essence of 'who you are' and a person's identity, we realise that personality is not just an internal process that an individual plays out daily but is impacted by external factors and has an impact on everyone and everything within that person's grasp.

In other words, personality is about internal processes as well as being partly an individual's link with the outside world. In a similar way, not only is personality affected by external factors, but personality itself can alter external factors e.g. we might argue that an outward exhibition of personality can come through an individual's subconscious body language. Body language as an indicator of personality can alter the course of a conversation between two people and cause it to flourish or break down (Ford, 2010, p.28, cf. Cole, 2016).

Academically, the term 'personality' is a multi-disciplinary topic which, before we progress to look at how personality changes, needs to explored fully to that we gain an understanding of the parameters that we are discussing and the development of the field. This will ensure that we are conversant in the terminology that will be used in the remainder of this book and the psychological, philosophical and historical advances that form our thinking and understanding today.

There are many different definitions of personality, which we will come to, however, each of these definitions relies on whether or not we believe in the idea of 'self' or 'psyche'. In other words, we might say, definitions rely on whether we believe there is something that makes us 'who we are' that is separate, but linked, to our physical being (Brunas-Wagstaff, 1998, cf. Farrell, 2010). Historically and theologically, this has been called the 'spirit' or the 'soul' (Vidal, 2011 cf. Mendy, 2013). The idea of personality, we might argue, relies on an understanding of the idea that the psyche, which is the conscious thinking, unconscious thinking, preferences and behaviour, is somehow separate from but linked to our physical being.

This is the idea that within the corpse, in which we stand, there is something that cannot be broken down in to cells, molecules, atoms, protons, neutrons or electrons. It is the idea that there is something in our bodies that cannot be dissected or seen under a microscope. We can enhance this further by simply thinking about a person's sexuality: under a microscope there is no concrete way of concluding if a person is heterosexual, homosexual, bisexual or any other sexual orientation definition that an individual gives him or herself. We cannot tell without doubt from a dissection, or an autopsy, if the individual is a person of faith (whether that be Christian, Muslim, Jewish, Buddhist, Sikh, Hindu or any other recognised or unrecognised religion). We cannot tell from a dissection of the physical body of a person whether they were kind and humble or harsh and boastful. Lastly, if we were to open up a person's heart there is no way we could possibly find love, compassion or even hatred.

In essence, by this definition there must be something in the chemistry and the neurology of our brains and body which we sometimes define as psyche, soul, personality or even 'self' which is intangible and transcends the physical state.

The idea of the psyche is not a modern one; indeed, it probably predates world religions by thousands of years because the idea of a soul or 'self' is central to all of the mainstream religions e.g. the Abrahamic religions are built on the notion that ordinary human beings can communicate with a higher entity and that the soul can become more like their god. Another example would be Buddhism which relies on seeking an inner peace and seeking knowledge from within and that the soul reincarnates and tethers itself to other physical frames.

Greek Philosophy

The idea of the psyche was central to Greek philosophy and is captured wonderfully in Plato's dialogue 'Phaedo' which is a hypothetical, imaginary Socratic discussion between characters who debate the immortality of the soul. According to Platonic thinking, the psyche brings life to whatever 'body' it inhabits; therefore, the soul brings life and is the opposite of death (Wagner, 2001, p.8). Smith (2010, p.91) puts it like this: 'For Plato, psyche is a universal principle in which individual humans participate by the very fact of their existence.' In other words, 'psyche', which in Platonic terms is about an ability to reason as well as identity, is linked to our human frame and because we are living we possess an individual personality and soul. Plato theorised that when we die the soul is somehow severed from the body since he interprets death as the soul's separation from the body. What is important to remember here is that Plato recognised that when an individual is alive they possess an intangible spirit which manifests itself in thought and reason (which both come in conscious and unconscious forms), behaviour and identity. However, when that individual dies, that sense of thought, reason, behaviour and identity is no longer linked to the physical frame of the body. Whether that soul is immortal is something which is somewhat irrelevant to our discussion.

Following out of this style of thinking, up to the Medieval times and the advent of modern medicine, this psyche or personality was seen to be affected by four internal humours, therefore, altering an individual's attitude and reason. It was seen that an illness or personality disorder was an imbalance of one of the four humours (Kelly, N., Rees, B. & Shuter, P., 2003). Galen, who was a Greek physician living between c.130-200 AD, hypothesised that the specific balance of these four humours an individual possesses determines their temperament (Galen, 1968). For instance, as Matthews, Deary and Whiteman (2009) summarise, Greek and Medieval thought stated that the possession of too much blood in the body would to lead towards a sanguine attitude of optimism and confidence. Too much phlegm in the body and the temperament would tend towards being stolid and calm. They believed that too much black bile not only led to physical illness but also led the psyche to state of depression. Thus, up until modern medicine, the theory that these four humours, in a certain balance, would form an individual's personality and temperament thrived.

Even though we have seen many scientific breakthroughs since the discovery of bacteria, and we possess an ever-expanding understanding of physical and mental health, and we might see the obvious flaws in the humours argument, there is also an element of truth. We understand that a person's personality can be influenced by chemicals such as serotonin and melatonin and an imbalance of these hormones can cause depression. (Altieri et al., 2013). Similarly, the misuse of drugs can have a lasting effect on the mind, reasoning and behaviour and therefore on the psyche (De Wit, 2005). Thus, similar to ancient thinking, we have an understanding that the 'self' is a fragile, intangible entity that can be affected by the tangible. In addition, we also note that in addition to this chemical effect the situation in which we find ourselves effects the personality. Our social context, economic context and even religious context are all catalysts that affect the formation and development of that notion of self which is somehow tethered to the human frame we adopt.

Post Enlightenment Philosophy

Thus far, we have established that personality is a complex formation of a combination of different factors which make a person 'who she or his is'. The complications then start when we look at two post-enlightenment schools' perspectives on the matter. Both Carl Jung and Sigmund Freud had very different ideas about the notion of personality and self.

Freud's developed ideas about personality are based on a threefold structure: 'id' (das Es), 'ego' (das Ich) and 'superego' (das Über-Ich) (Freud, 2016, pp.11-13). Some, at first glance, can be mistaken in believing that Freud's tripartite division of the psyche is comparable to Plato's division of the psyche into the appetites (or desires), the spirit and the conscious mind (Gallucci, 2001).

It would be naïve of us to think that there is no correlation between the philosophical their ideas since Freud even cites Plato in his writings on the subject (Silverman, 1985). However, Freud's ideas, as might be expected due to the time of writing, are far more developed even if they do originally stem from Plato.

The 'id' is, as Rennison (2015) describes, the state of mind we all possess at birth. It is the idea of 'a seething mass of wholly selfish desires and the impulses aimed at the immediate and complete gratification of those ideas' (Rennison, 2015). In a sense, it is the inherited unconscious primitive nature of humanity and its instincts as well as sexual desires. De Berg describes it beautifully and concisely like this:

"The id constitutes the lustful, aggressive (in Freud's terminology, sexual) art of our personality. It comprises both the pleasure-seeking urges with which we are born and the wishes, obsessions, and other affects derived from or associated with them. It is not a region of the mind, but a process made up of drives which are always operative, constantly pushing for satisfaction and constantly being pushed back (repression), diverted into cultural activities (sublimation), acted out (temporary satisfaction, or discharged in other ways (dreams, faulty actions). The id does not argue or deliberate,

possesses no values or rules and respects neither common sense nor logic. It is pure craving."
(De Berg, 2015, p.50)

Thus, Freud argues that this is the state in which we are born and then 'ego' and 'superego' subsequently develop. The 'ego' is the agency which seeks to reconcile the unrealistic and instinctive 'id' with reality. As Sandler describes: the ego is the decision-making part of mind which is seen as a 'coherent organisation of mental processes' (Sandler, 1997). Therefore, whilst the 'id' is unconscious, the 'ego' can be the conscious process of the mind or unconscious processes which, as Rennison (2015) points out, is the 'individual's [ability] to adapt to reality' and the 'exercise[d] control' over the impulsive 'id'.

Finally, Freud's third facet of the mind is the 'superego'. This is the idea that the mind has a part which is formed and continually develops because of the values, morals and, we could add, society's conventions, that we as humans take into consideration in our thought process. In reality, it is the 'internalised voice of parents, carers and society which provide the individual with the rules and regulations' (Rennison, 2015). Interestingly, in Freud's model the 'superego' can operate on a conscious level, with the ego's decision making process, or even unconsciously as it affects the ways we think and act in an automatic, instinctive way.

These three facets of the mind work in opposition and yet collaboration with each other to form what we would call 'the self' or the psyche. Freud notes that the 'id' is present from birth and then the 'ego' and 'superego' develop from it as an individual grows. He argues that these three components of the mind interact with each other and produce the personality which we adopt. The balance of these three components and the emphasis we give to each, in Freud's theory, determine what type of personality we possess. For instance, we might argue that an over emphasis on the 'superego' can produce anxiety since the individual falls short of its demands (Rennison, 2015) and when the 'id' demands are not fulfilled then it can cause 'unfocussed, neurotic anxiety' which might not register in the conscious mind of the individual (Rennison, 2015, p.105).

Jung, initially agreed with Freud, but then developed his own model for personality and the psyche. Similar to Freud, Jung developed a tripartite model. Firstly, Jung suggested that individuals possess an ego. This 'ego' is the conscious mind which is can be made up of perceptions, thoughts, feelings and memories that may enter consciousness. Engler (2013) states clearly that, for Jung, this ego is not the true centre of personality. In other words, this Jungian ego is the superficial elements of personality to which there is a 'personal unconscious' and 'collective conscious' that lies beneath the surface. Jung likens it to an island rising from the sea - some of the island is visible whilst some of it lies in the shallow waters and other parts lie in the depths of the sea. We might liken it to an iceberg: there is a visible element which is conscious, whilst there are hidden elements which are unconscious. The 'personal unconscious' element of the psyche is the 'perceptions, thoughts and feelings that are easily retrieved' or/and 'repressed or forgotten individual experiences' (Engler, 2013, p.67). In Jung's own terminology, the 'personal unconscious' is made up of the contents of that 'became unconscious either because it has lost its intensity and was forgotten or because... [the contents] is repressed' or it is mind content which never had enough intensity to reach the conscious mind but yet still forms part of the individual's psyche (Aziz, 1990, p.19).

The final component of Jung's theory is that of the 'collective unconscious'. It would be very easy and tempting to attempt to link Jung's 'collective unconscious' with Freud's 'superego' because from a first glance it is obvious that there are overlaps. However, the two phrases are not co-equal in meaning. The 'superego' is the idea of values and morals that might be taught or simply absorbed from society. On the other hand, Jung's 'collective unconscious' is the content of the mind that transcends the individual's 'personal unconscious' and Jungian ego. It is made up of that which is 'prior to personal experience' (Progoff, 2013, p.54) some of which could be inherited, impulsive and biological, which is most probably unconscious, and yet there could be parts (like moral and values) that are at times unconscious and yet sometimes enters in to the conscious mind. Thus, the phrase 'collected unconscious' can be misleading, but it is important to understand the spirit in which Jung used it.

For Jung, when you combine these elements, and they are bound together in one mind, they become the psyche, 'the self', or an individual's personality. However, Jung took his idea a step further than Freud to examine the balance between these three elements. To do this he developed his idea of preferences. Jung concluded that each person possesses four 'psychological functions': these are sensation, intuition, thinking and feeling (Quenk, 2009). These functions are focused on how we interact with the world around us. Meier (2010) describes how these four functions can be grouped into perception (meaning taking in information) and judgement (meaning how we make decisions). 'Sensation' is about perception, is about gathering 'concrete data' with our five senses. Intuition is about making 'connections' and deducing meanings beyond sensory experience (Jung, 1926). Jung then describes 'thinking' and 'feeling' as methods of evaluating, judging and making choices. He deliberates that 'thinking' is the application of objective and rational criteria which and 'feeling' is a method of evaluating considering what is important to the individual. Finally, Jung then presents the idea of two attitudes: the introversion and extraversion. Thus, what we can see is the start of a formulation of a set of scales that can be used to categorise and measure a person's personality: for instance, is an individual's preference more 'thinking' than 'feeling' or more 'extraverted' than 'introverted'?

Thus, for Jung, the psyche is more than just 'who we are' but is also, we might call, the outworking of 'who we are'. To develop Jung's idea and to attempt to define this outworking, we might say that the personality or the psyche (which is made up of the 'ego', the 'personal unconscious' and the 'collective unconscious') is shown internally as our beliefs, thought processes (conscious and unconscious), our understanding, knowledge, experiences, repressed memories, motivations and stream of consciousness. However, the personality can then manifest externally as behavioural functions such as conscious action and reaction, subconscious or automatic action and reaction, spoken and written word, body language and appearance.

Consequently, if we take Freud and Jung's ideas of the psyche we can see that, whatever theory we prefer, the personality is that sense of being that is at the core of each individual which is conscious and unconscious, the inherited impulses with which we are born and the external experiences and ideas to which an individual is subjected, as well as the outworking and tangible effects and reactions of all of the above. Of course, this relies on the idea that there is a true self - not necessarily one that is fixed and unchangeable but has a certain plasticity and ability to develop over time whether that be, in Freudian terms, the change of balance between the 'id' and 'the ego' and 'the superego', or, in Jungian terms, changes in preferences toward the psychological functions.

From this initial discussion of the psyche and the personality, we can obviously see how there are links to many aspects of everyday life. If we take the education setting as an example, we can see this clearly. First of all, in Freudian terms, a pupil or student learns in an educational setting which enhances their 'ego' and their 'superego'. In Jungian terms, a pupil or student's education will affect their thought process ('ego') as well as enhancing 'personal and collective unconsciousness'. For educators, the very personality they possess will give a different experience to the students in their care (Cooper, 2010, p.9, cf. Crozier, 2013). In Freudian terms, their tripartite psyche will influence and shape the way they teach as well the way the students will learn (Cooper, 2010, p.219). Yet, we might say, in Jungian terms, the educator's psyche is constantly being drawn upon by students: the 'ego', the 'personal consciousness' and the 'collective unconsciousness' are sources of energy for the students and inform and influence the methods which are used to teach skills or impart knowledge. Thus, different teachers possessing different psyches and personalities produces varying experiences for students (Kline, 2013, p.128).

Now that we have examined the historical thinking behind personality and before we can progress to look at how a personality might change, we need to look at some, relevant, modern day models of personality so that we understand the context and contemporary thinking on the subject.

The Psychodynamic Approach

The first theory and model we must look at in modern personality thinking is that of 'psychodynamics'. The psychodynamic model is the theory closest to that of Freud's philosophy.

Caligor, Kemberg and Clarkin (2007) describe personality as 'the dynamic [meaning constantly changing or evolving] organisation of enduring patterns of behaviour, cognition, emotion, motivation and ways of relating to others that are characteristic of an individual'. Wolitzky (2006) adds to this by stating that the psychodynamic model approaches personality as 'inner conflict' of conscious thought and, especially, the subconscious. Schacter et al. (2013) describe it as the strivings of 'forces that lie beneath awareness'. In psychiatry terms, treatment of psychological disorders then becomes the raising 'awareness' and 'resolution' of these conflicts (Wolitzky, 2006).

The Person-Centred Approach

Dr. Carl Rogers was an eminent psychologist, during the 1950s and 1960s, who had a passion for helping people to develop and grow, and thus, out of his work the idea of person-centred approaches to personality was formulated (Sharf, 2012). The theory that developed out of this his work is based on the following: each member of the population has a 'personality structure' that is unique to them.

This 'personality structure' is made up of 'multiple variables' within a person (Hampson, 2000, p.37). Of course, the actual names of these variables are up for discussion and debate with each personality assessment tool seemingly having a different set of variables. Central to this theory is the idea of self-concept and gaining a closer understanding of 'who you are' as an individual.

Gillon (2007) states that this sort of approach to personality suggests that there is a 'consistent version of personal identity' or in other words that an individual has an inner core personality which is not necessarily linked to external factors or influences. In essence, this theory states that our personalities affect the way in which we react, respond and adapt to external factors.

This sort of thinking does, of course, have pros and cons. Firstly, we can see that the idea of a consistent core of identity could display an element of truth because within each theory of personality there is an acknowledgement of certain factors which are building blocks of personality. However, what must be questioned is the 'consistency' of this core identity. Without wishing to delve into pure semantics, the term consistency implies that there is a sense of stability and fixed state. In others words, this theory looks at personality as a central core with an emphasis of personality affecting external factors more than personality being affected by external factors. Having said this, Rogers himself understood personality to have a certain fluidity and to be continually in progress (Wilkins, 2016). Within the spine of literature, there seems to be a level of uncertainty around this point. However, if we understand the development of the personality as a change in variables which then alters the identity to a new type of consistency then we might come to some sort of a resolution. Basic criticism of this model of personality comes from some who believe that it does not possess a strong enough theory of personality because it was initially a model of practising and counselling (Freeth, 2007).

In any case, there is an element in this theory that is extremely interesting. The person-centred approach is built on the premise that an analyst or therapist is more of a facilitator than a person with all the correct answers or understanding and that they can help a person overcome a psychological issue or disorder. The approach stresses, as explained by Gross (2015, p.88), 'as no one else can know how we perceive, we are the best experts on ourselves' (cf. Rogers, 1959). This means that the psychologist or personality assessment practitioner can facilitate discussion around personal and professional development using the results of personality assessment allowing the individual to forge his or her own way and develop in the way that is appropriate for the individual rather than trying to force an individual down a suggested pathway.

Cognitive-Behavioural Theory

The third school of personality theory is that which focuses on cognition and thought processes. In fact, subscribers to this school of thought completely discount Freudian psychoanalysis and psychodynamic thought.

Simply and concisely put, cognitive theory states that personality is constantly being formed by reaction and interaction with the world around the individual (Cervone & Pervin, 2015). In other words, thinking processes, in reaction to external stimuli, form 'who we are' and set in place patterns that we follow based on our own past experience. We might describe those thinking processes in terms of emotion, motivation and even memories (whether conscious or unconscious). Similarly, we might interpret 'external stimuli' as environmental factors, situational factors and the interaction with others in who enter our sphere (Cervone & Shoda, 1999). Of course, this is in opposition to Freudian psychodynamics and person-centred approaches because it apparent that it puts less emphasis on an inner-most state of being and more emphasis to the analysis of actions and thought process in determining and assessing personality. Whilst there might be some truth in the formation of personality as a response to behaviour and action (which in itself is a reaction to external stimuli), there are some issues with this theory which makes it less helpful to our study.

First of all, we might say that the theory does not, significantly enough, take into account that cognition and behaviour alone might not be enough to determine personality. By this we mean that personality might be made up of more than just reaction to external factors. Secondly, the model does not consider that some aspects of personality and some aspects of personal outlook on life might be formed internally through chemical processes. Thus, rather than external stimuli playing the main part in forming personality, it might be in balance with innate, biological features of the brain. That, of course, is not to say that the balance is equal in any way. Lastly, we might understand personality as the core of an individual which itself uses reactionary behaviour rather than always as a response to external factors.

We would highlight one point about personality and reactionary behaviour: is behaviour always part of a formation of personality and character or can it simply be an indicator of an already formed personality? Of course, a critical analysis reveals that the answer must be a mixture of both behaviour forming personality and that behaviour can be indicator of personality. Similarly, behaviour might be an indicator of personality that in turn has been formed by behaviour.

Trait Approaches

The final school of thought that we will discuss is that of 'trait' theory which is very close to Jungian thinking discussed earlier. Similar to cognitive theory, trait approaches to personality focuses on a set of variables which are built out of actions and characteristics. Eysenck, in his book 'Dimensions of Personality' (1950), theorised that there are 'specific responses' which are actions to a one-time specific situation. Carducci (2009) gives the example of when someone yells when they are angry at work. Then Eysenck goes on to describe 'habitual responses' - thus meaning that responses are repeated or become habit. Out of these actions, Eysenck then states that 'specific responses' and 'habitual responses' form traits (or, in other words, typical characteristics exhibited by an individual). Then his theory stated that a number of these traits put together form personality 'type'.

We can see how this understanding of personality would be extremely useful in a discussion around personality change. In our study, we might say that personality types and traits can be stripped back to 'specific responses' and 'habitual responses' and then discussed in an effort to allow us an understanding of how personality has changed.

The danger with this theory is when we get to the level where we discuss type. Although it might be useful to, at times, categorise individuals into a set number of personality types as does the Myers-Briggs Type Indicator (MBTI) (Briggs-Myers & Myers, 2010), we must question how useful that would be to ongoing professional development. Categorising an individual's traits into a set number of personality types might be seen as oversimplification and crude categorisation.

Admittedly, assessment tools such as the MBTI are mostly used in work situations at a recruitment level where it is attempting to see either if an individual's personality would be an asset to the company or department, or where best to place an individual in addition to what roles to give them - therefore, discussion of type might be of great use. However, in our discussions of personality change it is easy to see how this would just be crude categorisation of individuals.

Of course, there is also one other possible danger here that needs to be highlighted: do specific responses always lead to personality development? Some might argue that any reactionary behaviour is either an indicator of personality or an influencer for the formation of personality. However, we might argue that the truth is that sometimes behaviour might be unconnected from personality. One simple example might be when a person experiences a medical condition such as psychogenic dissociative amnesia whereby there is a 'breakdown in identity' and it is almost that a new, temporary persona is adopted by the individual and, thus, their reactionary behaviour to external stimuli is not matched to the type of behaviour they would have exhibited with similar external stimuli prior to the amnesia (Parkin, 2013, p.163). In essence, behaviour might be a one-time out of character action which bears no correlation to an individual's personality. On the other hand, critics might argue that that type of one-time behaviour is an exhibition of aspects of an individual's personality which lie dormant to the outside world or even hidden from the individual themselves.

A Unified Approach to Defining Personality

In an attempt towards a unified approach to personality theory, we can see the obvious benefits of taking one model and seeking to apply it to our understanding of personality change. However, each of the models discussed above does have an element of truth and holds additional relevant information that the others do not. The understanding that we will be taking forward will be based on trait theory with added elements of the other theories. The reasoning behind this is that this theory of personality allows us to understand, in a more concrete way, how personality is formed.

If we take the person-centred approach, which initially was a psychiatry counselling tool, we can see that the idea of 'multiple variables' that makes up 'personality structure' is extremely vague and perhaps better understood in terms of Jung's psychological functions or in terms of Freud's id, ego and superego.

If we take the ideas of psychodynamic theory which spell out a sense of inner conflict, we can see an element of relatability and that it would allow for the raising of awareness of inner conflict and thus discussions around development. However, the terminology used in the discussion of the theory of personality is not easily accessible and the theory may have, in some analysts' eyes, an over emphasis on sexuality (Coon & Mitterer, 2008).

The positives of psychodynamic theory can be seen in trait theory: analysis methods of trait theory focus on ways of interacting with the world at large as well as internal cognitive and psychological functions which can be used to discuss the main foci of psychodynamic theory (emotion, motivation and behaviour). The element of specific response and habitual responses being the building blocks of traits is a far more useful to discussion personality change since they breakdown personality into smaller facets of which each, in turn, can be examined and discussed in detail. In essence, personality, we are arguing, is a jigsaw of facets which when put together forms the innermost being.

Behavioural approaches to personality theory teaches us that, to some extent, our responses to the outside world are both indicators of our personality and influencers of our own personality. Thus, it is our belief that this combination of ideas based on trait theory gives the most accurate idea of the formation and development of personality. In addition, when we put these elements together we can find a useable model which will allow for assessment of personality change.

Now that we have established the meaning of personality that we will take forward, we can now proceed to examine some causes with which we can shine some light on personality change that individuals experience.

Chapter Two

CONSCIOUS TRAINING AND COACHING

Eliza's Elocution and Etiquette Lessons:
George Bernard Shaw's 'Pygmalion'
1913

"You have no idea how frightfully interesting it is to take a human being and change her into a quite different human being by creating a new speech for her. It's filling up the deepest gulf that separates class from class and soul from soul."
(Bernard Shaw, 2000, p.63).

In the humorous Edwardian play, Pygmalion, based on an ancient Greek myth, Professor Higgins takes on a bet. Eliza Doolittle, a flower seller with a Cockney accent, is described as 'so deliciously low' and 'so horribly dirty' (Bernard Shaw, 2000, p.29). Higgins, being a phonetics professor, takes on her plea for training and coaching in linguistics and etiquette. Eliza wants self-improvement and to talk more 'genteel' so that she may one day 'be a lady in a flower shop 'stead of sellin'' at the corner of Tottenham Court Road' (Bernard Shaw, 2000, p.26). The play satires class division, socio-economic status and shows the development, or bildungsroman narrative as we might call it, of Eliza's personality. By modifying the way that Eliza speaks, her whole persona changes over the course of the play and, in the end, she marries into an aristocratic family which is only possible because she is a different person than she was at the play's commencement. This is important to our study because it highlights our first area of exploration: training the personality and consequently modifying characteristics.

Bernard Shaw makes us picture a rather linear development. Eliza gradually and consciously learns new characteristics and abandons some of her own personal personality characteristics because she is taught how to fit in to a different class' social conventions. In essence, Eliza's rough edges are sanded down and she becomes far more socially acceptable (Lucia, 2013, p.192). For our study, this raises two questions: firstly, can a person consciously modify their personality? And, secondly, is it possible that this can be done subliminally ethically or, hypothetically, unethically?

Magison et al. (2014) highlight a few studies which have looked at how training has led to personality change: they note that cognitive behaviour therapy as an intervention most notably changes an individual's personality with regards to extraversion and neuroticism (cf. Clark et al., 2003). Magison et al. (2014) argue that their studies have shown that 'targeting core behaviours that underline personality traits with the goal of engendering new, healthier patterns of behaviour [become] automatized and manifest in changes in personality traits' (p.1142). In other words, personality can be altered by identifying key areas for change and practising new behaviour and this new style of behaviour then becomes the norm. In the words of trait theory, we can see how 'specific responses' might become 'habitual responses' and then as such develop personality traits (Eysenck, 1950 and Carducci, 2009).

We might put it another way: when we get a common cold, we have a number of symptoms. We know that science has not yet developed an antibiotic for killing the cold virus, so we treat these symptoms instead by taking a course of tablets, powders, lozenges and liquid medicine. Treating these symptoms remove the power the common cold virus has over us and allows us to continue with our lives until our bodies produce a new antibody and arm our immune system. Similarly, by changing the manifestations of personality, which are the perceivable behavioural actions and other visible traits (such as communication, understanding the social convention surrounding a situation), an individual's personality can be greatly altered. It is easy to see how this type of training could be done consciously and subliminally.

Hudson and Fraley (2015) attempted to clarify this type of research further. Over an intensive research program, Hudson and Fraley found that when personality traits and behavioural characteristics were practised in 'trait-relevant daily behaviour', training and coaching could 'catalyse [an individual's] ability to attain trait changes' (p.490). Their research looked at how people lacking 'socially desirable personality traits' (p.491) consciously were able to modify their behaviour resulting in self-improvement. Similarly, Roberts and Hudson (2014, p.70) noted that an individual's goals and motives and aspirations were just as important to changes in personality traits since they affect daily behaviour.

If we take these three studies, we can see that Bernard Shaw's character, Eliza, exemplifies all of the conditions required to consciously develop her personality through training and coaching. At the beginning of the play, Eliza possesses an understanding that she does not enjoy what she considers as socially acceptable behaviour, she has goals and aspirations which motivate her to seek training to modify her personality characteristics. In an everyday context, if an individual in an educational setting does not possess good communication skills but, by practising and looking at improving their communication skills, there is a relative result of a change in their extraversion and openness. Therefore, their personality has changed. Discussions held in a manner of coaching, mentoring or even performance management that use personality assessments as an initial spark for conversation highlights that an individual might be able to forge their own pathway of change and might alter some behaviours or, put in Eysenck's terminology, they might alter some of their specific and habitual responses. For instance, if they are a person who gets extremely angry in the workplace, then it is possible though coaching discussions using personality assessment as a basis to begin to work through some of the causes of this anger and subsequently change behaviour. This change in behaviour, if habitual, as Eysenck (1950) would say, would be an indicator that personality has changed.

There is one thing that none of the studies are able to reveal – are these modifications long lasting or short lasting? In other words, what we do not know is if the participants' personalities were permanently affected or whether we might categorise the training episode and a short honeymoon period that follows as a digression from the norm and that they will return to their default personality characteristics over time. However, we might argue that if 'habitual responses' are modified by the training process then personality change is more than likely longer lasting.

Of course, subliminal training of personality traits is an almost elusive topic. Hypothetically disregarding ethics for the moment, subliminal training has been used successfully to modify people's personalities on mass. We need not look further than indoctrination for numerous examples. However, here is another form of subliminal training of personality characteristics: we have established that behaviour and personality traits are closely linked and therefore we can see how Pavlov's theory of classical conditioning of behaviour is extremely relevant.

Ivan Pavlov looked at how an event or a series of events could act as a stimulus and, as a result, trigger responses in behaviour (Kalat, 2010, p.200). For example, many people have a fear of the dentist. They have either heard horror stories or have experienced pain at a visit, therefore, when having to attend the dentist they automatically present signs of perhaps sweating, nervous heart-rate, heightened awareness and shaking. What has happened here is that they have been conditioned and they have been subliminally taught that a visit to the dentist coincides with pain. This conditioning can even extend further so that the person can be effected even before attending: when a reminder to attend an appointment finds its way into their mail, and they notice it, their symptoms can start. There are other countless examples we could give of classical conditioning. However, if we take this theory and apply it to personality traits we can see clearly how conditioning, which is a form of training whether it is voluntary or involuntary, could affect an individual's personality characteristics.

To take an example, if a person were physically abused repeatedly by the same attacker then their behaviour would be modified. Let us say that the victim of this abuse was helpless under the strength of the repeat attacker. At first, the victim might struggle and try to overpower the attacker. However, over time they might have learned and thus been trained to know that they cannot overpower their attacker and thus they remain still to receive the blow that always comes with this series of attacks knowing that it will be over quicker if they do not retaliate. The visible signs of change here are the behavioural changes – the victim has learnt not to respond. However, we can see how this might also be indicative of personality change: the repeated attacks and feelings of helplessness at the moment of the attack will have lasting effect and spill over to other areas of life. The victim's self-confidence and sense of helplessness and extraversion in other areas situations are likely to be modified. Their depressive thoughts and dread and anticipation for the next attack might hang like a shadow over them making them more introverted, sensitive to the comments of others and, perhaps, even unable to control pent-up anger: in effect, their cognitive function has been modified. We might argue that after seeking support relating to these repeated attacks, the victim's personality will still be deeply marred by the whole negative effect of conditioning and training they have experienced and might find it extremely difficult to return to the personality characteristics they possessed before the attacks.

It might also be possible for an individual to return to possess some desired personality characteristics because of this training. However, we would argue that they will never be able to return to their former personality entirely. This then begins to give us an answer as to whether or not training and coaching can produce lasting personality change.

To conclude this chapter, we have seen how training and coaching can affect personalities in very tangible and visible ways through modifying behaviour and cognitive function. Using Eliza's story as our inspiration, we have been able to analyse research literature to see how training and coaching can help with perceived self-improvement through the development of desirable personality traits. We have seen how training and conditioning, whether volitional or subliminal, can also produce changes in personality characteristics not only in positive ways but also in negative ways. This leads us nicely on to our second area of exploration of the reasons behind personality change.

Chapter Three

RELIGIOUS CONVERSION

Saul's Conversion from 'Acts of the Apostles'
c.80-90 AD

¹Meanwhile, Saul was still breathing out murderous threats against the Lord's disciples. He went to the high priest ²and asked him for letters to the synagogues in Damascus, so that if he found any there who belonged to the Way, whether men or women, he might take them as prisoners to Jerusalem. ³As he neared Damascus on his journey, suddenly a light from heaven flashed around him. ⁴He fell to the ground and heard a voice say to him,
"Saul, Saul, why do you persecute me?"
⁵"Who are you, Lord?" Saul asked.
"I am Jesus, whom you are persecuting," he replied. ⁶"Now get up and go into the city, and you will be told what you must do."
(Acts 9:1-6)

¹⁹ᵇSaul spent several days with the disciples in Damascus. ²⁰At once he began to preach in the synagogues that Jesus is the Son of God. ²¹All those who heard him were astonished and asked, "Isn't he the man who raised havoc in Jerusalem among those who call on this name? And hasn't he come here to take them as prisoners to the chief priests?" ²²Yet Saul grew more and more powerful and baffled the Jews living in Damascus by proving that Jesus is the Messiah.
(Acts 9:19b-22).

The story of 'Damascene Conversion' in the New Testament demonstrates our next type of personality change that we will examine. Saul's conversion appears in three places in the sacred Christian texts: it appears in third person narrative in 'Acts of the Apostles' chapter 9, in quoted speech in 'Acts of the Apostles' chapter

22 and in first person narrative in the 'Epistle to the Galatians' chapter 1. The purpose of these accounts each time is show a complete change in the personality of a character: Saul is transformed by a religious conversionary experience from a Christian hunter and persecutor to one of Christianity's most important advocates who is said to have written more than a third of the New Testament. Paloutzian et al. (1999) highlight similar accounts, such as that of St. Augustine of Hippo who from his own admission 'instantly felt a serenity in his heart and the darkness and doubt that he felt vanished' and he describes himself as being delivered from a life of debauchery and drunkenness. Both St. Paul and St. Augustine's experiences could be described as 'revelations' or 'epiphanies'.

Of course, it would be a mistake to simply view religious conversion as just an archaic notion and we must state that it is far from exclusive to Christianity: Paloutzian et al. (1999) draw attention to the Islamic conversion of Malcolm X in the late 1940s and we might supplement this example with Muhammad Ali's conversion to Islam, William Booth's conversion and the roots of the Salvation Army and Billy Graham's conversion to Christianity and his evangelical 'soul-saving' missions.

In each of these examples, the individual has experienced a transformation of character, possesses a new outlook on life and its events, and thus their personalities have undergone a lasting, enduring change because they have a fresh adherence to a new religious or moral code. Broughton & Ten Napel (2000) have even completed research which demonstrates that this change in moral code adherence and, by extension, modification of personality characteristics changes belief, can manifest itself in changes in political adherence and then manifest itself in electoral behaviour. In addition, in each of the above examples and in countless others, the individual's transformation of personality also is linked to a sense of proselytisation. Put another way, once the individual experiences what they consider to be a life-changing experience there is a tendency to want others to join them.

The research literature is particularly sparse on this topic and, when we analyse it, we can see that there are a few key points missing and questions that are never considered. The research that has been completed that links religious conversionary experience with personality change always seems to focus on dramatic change or an individual trigger event that suddenly alters the convert's personality. Paloutzian et al. (1999, p.1049) call this 'the stereotype of profound change', however, their research does not then go onto consider that personality change and religious conversion can be a much longer and subtler process.

Firstly, if a person has grown up and has been taught the teachings of their religion and then over time chooses to either adhere closer to the ideological beliefs or to weaken their links with these teachings, we must argue that personality characteristics would be modified. We say this because a change in beliefs has occurred and thus the individual's outlook, behaviours and actions would experience a change - however minute the change or modification of their personality traits might be. Freudian followers would explain this as a change in the 'superego' (Freud, 2016). For example, a Jewish youngster who has grown up in their faith and at the age of 12 or 13 receives teaching in preparation for their Bar/Bat Mitzvah is likely to experience a longer process of developing change to personality characteristics as they understand and take on the beliefs of their denomination more clearly. This change is still a religious conversionary experience, even though the individual has not changed religion and there has not been a singular event or 'light-bulb' moment whereby a sudden change of character has occurred.

Secondly, we must also consider that personality change is a life-long process and thus we must also consider that a longer process of closer adherence that might happen after a dramatic experience of conversion. In the Christian world, this is called a path of discipleship (Bonhoeffer, 2015, p.17) or holiness (Geiger et al., 2012, p.74) meaning that the individual's life might have dramatically changed in the past, and thus there is likely to have been a personality transformation, but the rest of their life is devoted to becoming closer to the ideal that they consider to be demonstrated by scripture and thus their personality continues to adapt. Therefore, personality change caused by religious conversion can be a lifelong process. Similarly, Islam and Judaism both have comparable notions: they consider conformation to scriptural laws, prayer and study of sacred texts a process of growing closer to their respective gods and thus the development of the 'soul'. We might here note that similar processes can be seen in cults (Taylor, 2006, p.44). (The discussion of cults has been given greater consideration under the chapter on political change and indoctrination).

Thirdly, religious conversion can work the opposite way. Instead of a believer's personality growing closer to the beliefs as demonstrated by their sacred texts, social conventions and taught by figures of authority in their communities, a believer can also change from strong adherence to their faith to agnosticism or to atheism (Hirst, 2010, p.155). When we consider this, we understand that such changes, no matter whether they are long developing processes or sudden 'changes of heart', will undoubtedly effect the individual's personality characteristics and traits.

Fourthly, a question we must ask is regarding the relationship between personality change and the forced conversion. In some countries and in some communities, there is a very deep sense of pressure to conform to specific religious identities. For instance, let us say that a couple wish to marry, however, one of the couple does not identify himself/herself to the religion of their partner's family and community. In order to proceed with the marriage, it is possible that the individual will either feel pressure to conform and convert or, as has happened in some cases, is forced to convert. When this occurs, there is undoubtedly going to be some type of change in personality. However, it is obvious that these changes will be completely different to those experienced by those who voluntarily have converted to the religion because of a change in beliefs and, perhaps, morals. We might suggest that forced conversion can cause characteristics such as insecurity, the desire to conform and even introversion to develop. However, this is a gap in the literature and, until there are studies that specifically look at this, we can but make informed predictions and educated guesses.

When we consider these points, we can see how personality change linked to religious conversion is not as simple as first thought or as it is presented in much of the research literature. We can also see how the idea of revelation can indirectly affect teaching. We keep this idea of adherence to beliefs or a change in beliefs in our minds as we move on to consider mental illness and instability as a reason behind personality change.

Chapter Four

MENTAL ILLNESS AND INSTABILITY

Sylvia Plath's 'The Bell Jar'
1963

"If neurotic is wanting two mutually exclusive things at one and the same time, then I'm neurotic as hell. I'll be flying back and forth between one mutually exclusive thing and another for the rest of my days."
(Plath, 2005, p.90).

An Extract from Sylvia Plath's Unabridged Journals
Friday, June 20th, 1958

"...It is as if my life were magically run by two electric currents: joyous and positive and despairing negative; whichever is running at the moment dominates my life, floods it. I am now flooded with despair, almost hysteria, as if I were smothering."
(Plath, 2000, p.395).

Mental instability is a very complex notion: it is often not visible and thus it is commonly misunderstood. However, it is a significant cause of personality change. Sylvia Plath was an American poet and author whose work and journals bear the unmistakeable hallmark of a person suffering with what is now known as bipolar disorder. In her writings, she soul-searches and attempts to explain her feelings of stages of depression that are counter-acted by charged manic stages. She describes it as being 'run by two electric currents' (Plath, 2000, p.395). In Plath's case, her mental illness gave way to creativity at times and darkest depression at other times. We might describe her as oscillating between two sets of personality traits, behaviours and characteristics. In her semi-autobiographical novel, 'The Bell Jar', Plath utilises a metaphor for these two different of personalities she possesses: she imagines that, above her head, there is a glass bell jar. When the bell jar is lifted she is able to breathe, to act, to think clearly, to be happy and thus certain personality characteristics are manifested and demonstrated by her behaviour. However, when that glass bell jar is lowered, she feels trapped and starved of oxygen, suffocating from the inability to be understood and thus she demonstrates a different set of personality characteristics and traits (Plath, 2005). This metaphor appears time and time again during the course of the novel in different guises. A month after publishing her novel, Plath committed suicide because of the inability to cope with what she considered as her two personalities. In other words, Plath was unable to cope with the frequent, oscillating personality changes that she had endured for the most of her life.

Bipolar disorder is just one example of mental illness and when we look at other examples we can see that there are great differences between their effects on personality and how they affect the individual. Mental illnesses such as Schizophrenia, when they develop and are treated, can all, arguably, produce lasting results whereby an individual's personality can be changed for the rest of their lives. (Daly & Sand, 2012, pp.3-4). Whilst the same might be true of Postnatal Depression, Seasonal Affective Disorder (SAD), Obsessive Compulsive Disorder (OCD), Anorexia Nervosa and other mental disorders, treatment and correction of chemical imbalances (such as melatonin, serotonin and other such hormones) in the body might restore a person back, more or less, to their original personality or to a state of what might be considered as a 'healthier' set of personality traits and string of consciousness.

It might be argued by some that mental illness's effect on personality is not that it changes personality characteristics but that it gives dormant tendencies and traits, that are usually hidden, more emphasis and that inhibitors in our brains do not act in the same way as they have done previously. Thus, an individual would manifest stronger characteristics. However, any such shift in characteristics can, arguably, produce profound a personality shift whether this is temporary or has lasting effects (Freeth, 2007, p.60).

It would be naïve to think that mental instability (or any other cause of personality change) only affects the one individual. Since, as human beings, we do not live in individual silos devoid of any compassion or any link to the outside world, the mental illness of those we love and care for is almost certainly going to affect those of us who live in close proximity or have regular dealings with them (Hinshaw, 2007, p.3). The mental illnesses of others can, we might argue, adjust or affect our own personality traits. If we take Plath as our example once again, upon attempting and subsequently successfully committing suicide, we not only can we chart the personality changes in Plath but cannot dismiss the obvious psychological personality effects that this event and Plath's preceding stages of bipolar disorder would have had on her young children whom were present at the time of her suicide.

In the idea of personality assessment leading to discussion and perhaps even prompting professional and personal development, there is something we might learn from these points on mental illness. Our own personalities affect those around us.

Although an extreme situation, Plath's behaviour resulting from her personality had lasting effect on her family. Similarly, as we understand from our study of the definitions of personality, our personalities are affected by external factors as well as being an influencer on external factors. We can see how individuals are not only influenced by external forces but are influencers of external forces at one and the same time (Cervone & Pervin, 2015). Consequently, in the workplace, an individual's personality will be influenced by the external and environmental factors of their workplace as well as influencers of personalities in their sphere of influence.

This topic is incredibly important because it highlights that we are all prisoners of our own experiences and thus might have seen negative personality changes as well as positive changes.

During this chapter, we have focused on mental health's effects on personality and chemical triggers for changes. However, it is also important that we now look at trauma of both a physical and mental type and its effect on personality.

Chapter Five

T R A U M A

'Septimus Warren Smith' from Virginia Woolf's 'Mrs. Dalloway'
1925

*"The violent explosion which made Mrs. Dalloway jump and Miss Pym go
to the window and apologise came from a motor car which had drawn to the
side of the pavement precisely opposite Mulberry's shop window…
Everyone looked at the motor car. Septimus looked. Boys on bicycles sprang
off. Traffic accumulated. And there the motor car stood, with drawn blinds,
and upon them a curious pattern like a tree, Septimus thought, and this
gradual drawing together of everything to one centre before his eyes, as if
some horror had come almost to the surface and was about to burst into
flames, terrified him. The world wavered and quivered and threatened to
burst into flames… People must notice; people must see. People, she
thought, looking at the crowd staring at the motor car; the English people,
with their children and their horses and their clothes, which she admired in
a way; but they were "people" now, because Septimus had said, "I will kill
myself"; an awful thing to say. Suppose they had heard him? She looked at
the crowd."*
(Woolf, 2013, pp.11-13).

When published in the inter-war era, Virginia Woolf's novel,
Mrs. Dalloway, was considered scandalous. Throughout the book,
Clarissa Dalloway, the main protagonist, highlights themes of
feminism and homosexuality as well as mental illness. However, Mrs.
Dalloway is an intriguing book since it has two narrative threads that
run parallel over the course of the book. Therefore, running alongside
the narrative of Mrs. Dalloway's preparations for hosting a party is
the harrowing story of Septimus Warren Smith, a former soldier from
the First World War, who suffers from what was known as 'shell

shock' but is now known as 'Post-Traumatic Stress Disorder' (PTSD). The novel's first scene introduces us to Septimus' character when there is an explosion which comes from a motor car which causes a flood of battlefield memories to saturate his thinking and render him so anxious, nervous and confused that he wants to escape from the person he has become (Woolf, 2013, pp.11-13).

Thus, from Septimus' character, we can derive our next reason for personality change: trauma. Trauma might be a single event or it might have been longer developing and originating from a series of traumatic events. Similarly, we must define what we mean by trauma: we use trauma to mean a sense of distress and disturbance following an ordeal of suffering. This trauma might be physical or emotional. For instance, examples of trauma might be a severe vehicle accident, strokes, head injury and Post-Concussion Syndrome, Amnesia, sexual abuse (including rape and molestation), child abuse (including neglect, sexual assault, physical assault), emotional abuse, domestic abuse (including effects on the victim, assailant, witnesses and family life) and modern day slavery and trafficking.

Fisher and Van De Kolk (2015, pp.127-128) suggest that trauma and the fear that follows can 'drive' personality changes. In other words, a traumatic experience can suddenly alter an individual's personality. However, the feelings of fear, anger and shame that commonly follow trauma, linked with the mind's uncanny ability to replay events of trauma over and over again, can also continue the process of personality change. Consequently, trauma that might have happened years ago might be still affecting an individual's personality characteristics, thought processes and behaviour. Just like in Woolf's example of Septimus, trauma has an ongoing, lasting effect which can then lead to mental illness and borderline personality disorders (Chu, 1998, p.42). In addition, in cases of childhood trauma, especially of a sexual nature, personality changes could manifest many years later because of lack of understanding. We mean by this that the personality changes experienced by a victim of child abuse might be delayed and have a more profound effect when the victim is older and realises the severity and understands the nature of the attack(s) better. Countless examples have been given over the years whereby children were sexually assaulted by family members and never realised that what was going on was unacceptable and socially and morally wrong because they thought that this was the way all families lived. Then at a later date when they learn of the criminal nature of the trauma and consider it as abuse, more profound changes to personality can be exemplified by the individual as they start to understand.

Therefore, an event such as the ones listed above or a combination/series of events like these can profoundly affect a person's life by immediately modifying (Dolan-Sewell, 2001, p.93) or distorting (Derksen et al., 1999, p.71) the character traits they possess (such as openness to others, confidence, extroversion) or doing the same over a longer period of time and perhaps with a delay. Depending on the nature of the trauma and the disposition of the individual, these effects that manifest themselves in behavioural characteristics and, therefore, in an individual's personality, change might be only temporary or possess a lasting effect. In other words, the severity of the trauma, and the way that each individual deals with the trauma, will cause significant differences in the way their personalities change.

This shows us that the personality is a very susceptible to external influence and vulnerable to change. This also emphasises that training and coaching the personality, post trauma, might stabilise an individual's personality traits or produce socially desirable changes that deliver the individual to a healthier state of mind.

We have discussed trauma as some catastrophic events in an individual's life. However, trauma, for a teacher in an educational setting might be of a different nature. For instance, if an individual has been bullied in the workplace, then their personality might have become a lot more introverted and their outlook on life might be rather negative.

Now that we have outlined trauma as an initiator of personality change, we need to look at the way political ideological thought and changes in alignment with different political ideals can produce personality changes.

Chapter Six

POLITICAL ALLEGIANCE AND MORAL PERSPECTIVE AMENDMENT

Rev. John Newton: Gaoler of Slaves to Abolitionist Advocate
1831

"During this time I was engaged in the slave trade, I never had the least scruple as to its lawlessness. I was, upon the whole, satisfied with it, as the appointment providence had marked out for me; yet it was, in many respects far from eligible. It is, indeed, accounted as a genteel employment, as is usually very profitable, though to me it did not prove so, the Lord seeing that a large increase in wealth could not be good for me. However, I considered myself as a sort of gaoler or turnkey; and I was sometimes shocked with an employment that was perpetually conversant with chains, bolts, and shackles. In this view I had often petitioned, in my prayers, that the Lord, in his own time, would be pleased to fix me in a more humane calling... My prayers were now answered, though in a way I little expected. I now experienced another sudden, unforeseen change of life."
(Newton, 1831, p.108).

John Newton's story is a well-known tale of redemption and an attempt for an individual to put right the injustice of the Nineteenth Century's 'Slave Trade'. In his own words, above, Newton illustrates a change in political and moral perspective which we can attribute to a change in personality too. Being a former Royal Navy sailor, Newton became the captain of slave ship trafficking human cargo for exploitation. After spiritual conversion to Christianity, he still continued his practise until he felt conviction to support the Abolitionist movement and a sense of guilt regarding his former conduct. We can see, in Newton's personality change, obvious links to his religious conversion but then subsequent personality changes that highlight that personality change is not static and not a one-time event but rather that it can be a dynamic, gradual set of changes or modifications to an individual's psyche. We know of Newton's first set of changes (religious conversion) which are proceeded by political and moral changes which then affect his personality characteristics, traits and behaviour (Newton, 1831, p.108).

Newton's story highlights a very ancient idea of penitence and change in behavioural action: ancient Greek, Hellenistic culture and subsequent philosophers and theologians have called this 'metanoia' (μετάνοια) (Strong, 2009). Personality and psychology literature highlight that political and moral thought (meaning what an individual considers to be right and of best interest) to be linked to personality predisposition (Mondak, 2010, p.122). Therefore, if a person undergoes a change in this predisposition or a process of 'metanoia' then politics and political thought are simply manifestations of a changed personality and behavioural characteristics.

We can expand on Mondak's work further by considering that a changing political or moral 'zeitgeist' means that not only could this effect a single individual but could result in group, demographic specific or mass-population changes in personality. In other words, changes in personalities might be replicated between individuals and the effects of one individual's change in perspective, which in turn modifies their personality, can ripple out to affecting those in close relationships with them or who work and interact with them. This is incredibly important because it highlights that making a positive impact by individuals self-modifying their own personality characteristics and behavioural action might subsequently spread to other individuals and those who interact with them.

Interestingly, in our discussion of Newton's political changes we have only discussed conscious changes in political and moral perspectives which affect personality characteristics. At this point, we need to highlight the darker side of political change. By this we do not mean a change of political allegiance to extremist views or to political standpoints that are considered by many to be unfavourable, we mean that across history we have seen subliminal attempts to indoctrinate the general public or a specific demographic that results in a modification of their thoughts on a matter, the modification of their actions and thus the modification of their personality characteristics. Let us take two different examples.

The first example is that of the growth of the Third Reich and the collapse of the Weimar Government in inter-war Germany. The Nazi party employed the trusted Dr. Joseph Goebbels with the sole purpose of being in charge of propaganda and spreading the Nazi message (Cull et al., 2003, p.150). He co-ordinated what we would now consider to be intensive campaigns to bring a right-wing ideal of Aryanism to become a normality and a view shared by the masses (Herf, 2014, p.94). Along with other members of the Nazi party, he helped modify the views of ordinary men, women and children. It is unfair to say that anti-Semitism was not present in Germany in the shadow of the First World War, however, propaganda was used virulently to spread the message against Jews. Not only were their posters and speeches but there were co-ordinated book burnings of non-Aryan materials, films like 'The Eternal Jew' (Der Ewige Jude, 1940) which was a faux documentary, children's books like 'Der Giftpliz' which taught how to recognise Jews from their fellow Germans (Hiemer, 1938), pogroms, ghettoization and subsequent concentration and extermination camps. We, in hindsight, can question whether, without the escalation of this indoctrination, if the Holocaust would have happened and by extension we can surmise that political, moral and even racial perspectives were modified and thus people's personalities were changed subliminally and, at times, consciously by their own volition (Lee, 2005, p.32) and this produced devastating results.

The second example is that given by the American Psychological Association. Dittmann (2002) outlines the story of Kerry Noble who was a leading member of a cult known as the 'Covenant, Sword and Arm of the Lord'. The cult had developed an anti-Semitic message, a homophobic stance and a standpoint against civil rights.

In 1984, upon arriving at a church with a large homosexual following with a briefcase of explosives, he had intended on setting the timing mechanism and leaving. However, upon realising that 'his enemy appeared no different from anyone else' he decided that what he was about to do was morally wrong and left the building without causing harm. Dittmann presents this as an indicator of 'brainwashing' (Dittmann, 2002, p.30) and thus evidence of indoctrination.

Looking analytically at this, we can identify two different types of possible indoctrination: a traditional approach to indoctrination, that is an intended thought and behaviour modification from someone in authority, and secondly, self-indoctrination, meaning that an individual indoctrinates themselves in the process of indoctrinating others with their ideology. We can illustrate this further by simply quoting an often-used phrase: 'he is beginning to believe in his own lies'. By this we mean that in preaching their ideology it is possible for an individual to make themselves believe virulently in the ideas they are espousing. Barnes (2007) calls this 'self-deception' leading to 'interpersonal deception'. In Noble's case, he was the victim of traditional indoctrination received from the cult, but as one of its' leaders he was one in authority who was indoctrinating others and in the process started to believe more intensively in the ideology he was exhibiting. Thus, we can establish that Noble's personality change was caused by an indoctrinating political, racial and moral standpoint which was then intensified by his own preaching of the ideology.

Noble's story also identifies how indoctrination and thus a change of political allegiance and moral perspective amendment is not always permanent since upon arriving at church he was again transformed and his personality changed – whether that was because of a sense of compassion for others or a simple realisation of the apparent absurdity of the ideology he aligned himself with, we do not know. Nevertheless, by his subsequent actions of not causing harm when he had fully intended to cause harm to those who were different from himself and then consequently speaking at conferences to 'speak out on the effects of mind control and destructive cults' proves that characteristics of his personality had most certainly changed.

Political allegiance amendment also can come in another form: members of political parties who defect to another political party because of policy preferences or because of a change of ideal might be examples of personality change within governmental organisation. We must air caution here though, a change of political party does not necessarily mean that an individual has modified their political perspective and thus demonstrate a characteristics of personality change – a defection to another political party might be for purely reputational gain, economic and financial support for upcoming campaigns, or that the party they are defecting to have become a closer representation of that person's inherent ideals and values.

In concluding of this chapter, we have seen how effective and how efficient changes in political views and moral standpoints can be in altering an individual's personality and that then can manifest itself in visible, behavioural and audible ways. We have noted how the external influences as well as internal influences can profoundly modify personality.

Chapter Seven

MEMORY DEGENERATION AND ALZHEIMER'S DISEASE

Jake's Degeneration in Samantha Harvey's 'The Wilderness' 2010

"He looks around his car and tries to remember what make it is; he cannot. He opens the window to feel what month it is. It isn't a month. There aren't months. There are just happenings, a lack of signposts ... He pulls up at the side of the road, lifts his glasses, and rubs his eyes. He has been doing this journey to and from work every day for thirty-five years. He pores over the map."
(Harvey, 2010, pp.26-27).

"When he looks in the mirror he does not see an old man, nor does he see a brain that lacks logic. He sees himself, greatly changed, but undeniably himself..."
(Harvey, 2010, p.43).

"For the finest shard of the time he believes that he has had his life and that it is over and a panic grips him because he cannot remember a thing, not a thing, he has had it and lost it, or it has lost him."
(Harvey, 2010, p.328).

'The Wilderness' is a touching novel which charts Jake Jameson's later life and the onset of Alzheimer's Disease. Over the course of the novel, Jake's character and personality change. His behaviour and attitudes to everyday life events become blurred and confused and he becomes unrecognisable to the person he once was. Not only does he not recognise himself physically, but he is unable to recognise his personality characteristics. He looks and acts like a different person – a person he does not know. The above quotations from the novel show the gradual deterioration of his memory over time and inability to hold onto his identity. The novel begins and he is having trouble remembering his way home from his place of work as an architect (Harvey, 2010, pp.26-27) and, over the development of the text, his personality changes so much so that he is unable to remember anything about himself, his likes and dislikes or even his own thought processes (Harvey, 2010, p.328). This illustration highlights, for us, our next area of discussion surrounding personality change: memory loss and long-term memory illnesses.

Long term illnesses and memory difficulties are often heralds of personality change. Unlike some of the other areas, we have discussed this area can be far more gradually developing. Alzheimer's Disease is but one example of Dementia and thus only one example of memory degeneration causing an irreversible change in personality. Other examples include Huntington's Disease (which is a hereditary condition in which the brain's ability to cope with emotions, feelings, general cognitive functions and physical functions are gradually forgotten) and also the development of brain tumours.

Mahoney et al. (2011) conducted a research study which attempted to measure changes in personality linked with frontotemporal lobar degeneration. The study utilised a multi-method data collection methodology: a questionnaire completed by a primary care giver, who had known the participant for ten years, who was then able to answer a series of questions based on the participant's current personality traits and the traits they exhibited ten years previously. The second method was the use of magnetic resonance imaging (MRI) scans. The results were then compared. The study found that participants had become less extraverted, exhibited less agreeableness, less conscientiousness and less openness. The results also showed an increase in the participants' neuroticism (Mahoney et al., 2011). According to their findings this pattern in the changes of personality were linked to brain architectural changes and cognitive functionality. There are, of course, some areas in the methodology utilised by Mahoney et al. which are not ideal for ensuring accuracy of results: for instance, asking a relative or primary care giver about degenerative changes that begun ten years ago is particularly an issue since it is a temptation to look back with rose-tinted spectacles on how the participant used to be and thus they may overstate the changes to personality. However, if we compare this with a few similar studies we get surprisingly similar results.

Pocnet et al. (2013) completed an extremely similar study looking at personality changes in patients suffering from a mild form of Alzheimer's Disease. In this study, they asked patients themselves to complete a personality assessment questionnaire looking at their current traits and the traits they exemplified five years previously. Similar results were found linking memory degeneration to introversion and increased neuroticism and decreased openness. These results can also be replicated further: if we look at Talassi et al. (2007) traits such as talkativeness and quietness, ability to reason and being 'out of touch' with reality are linked to the same type of results as Pocnet et al. (2013) and Mahoney et al. (2011). We could continue comparing numerous studies that have found these changes in traits as patterns in personality change, however, we can summarise them by simply stating that, on the whole, primary care givers and Alzheimer's Disease patients themselves notice profound change in personality characteristics and behavioural traits.

On the other hand, there are also other two other points that need to be made here. Firstly, it has been discovered that some personality traits increase 'resilience' to Alzheimer's Disease and thus, in turn, can changes in personality through memory deterioration and frontotemporal lobar degeneration. Terracciano et al. (2013) conducted a research project that took participants from a pool of 519. These participants had enrolled in an autopsy program and as such completed and recompleted a number of personality assessments over a period of years.

A number of these patients died without mental impairment, however many developed clinical dementia – some had even developed it before they could complete a personality assessment for the first time. After their death, their personality assessments, clinical notes regarding mental impairment and brains were examined. The study was able to note that there was significant evidence to state some personality profiles can be 'associated with lower risk or delay of clinical dementia' and, as a result, a resilience towards personality changes caused by memory degeneration.

Secondly, similar types of changes in personality traits and characteristics to those experienced by Alzheimer's Disease patients have been found in other types of memory deterioration sufferers. It has been found that depression, alcohol abuse, dehydration and the side effects of medicines can cause memory degeneration which in turn changes personality traits and behavioural characteristics (De Wit, 2005, p.259). These types of issues which affect the memory, which seem less intrusive, can be reversible (Stringer et al., 2015, p.191) or can lead to more serious diseases, such as Mild Cognitive Impairment (MCI) (Spar & La Rue, 2007, p.36). This highlights that personality traits and behavioural characteristics might be early indicators of future memory degeneration and subsequent personality changes due to frontotemporal lobar deterioration. This bring us nicely to our next area of study: substance abuse and addictions as a cause for personality change.

Chapter Eight

SUBSTANCE ABUSE AND OTHER ADDICTIONS

Thomas De Quincey's 'Confessions of an English Opium Eater'
1821

"During the season of hope and redundant happiness which succeeded (that is, from eighteen to twenty-four) it [a painful affliction of the stomach] had slumbered; for the three following years it had revived at intervals; and now, under unfavourable circumstances, from depression of spirits, it attacked me with a violence that yielded to no remedies but opium." (De Quincey, 1873, p.18).

"...I now pass to what is the main subject of these latter confessions, to the history and journal of what took place in my dreams, for these were the immediate and proximate cause of my acutest suffering. The first notice I had of any important change going on in this part of my physical economy was from the reawakening of a state of eye generally incident to childhood, or exalted states of irritability. I know not whether my reader is aware that many children, perhaps most, have a power of painting, as it were upon the darkness, all sorts of phantoms... For this and all other changes in my dreams were accompanied by deep-seated anxiety and gloomy melancholy, such as are wholly incommunicable by words. I seemed every night to descend, not metaphorically, but literally to descend, into chasms and sunless abysses, depths below depths, from which it seemed hopeless that I could ever reascend. Nor did I, by waking, feel that I had reascended." (De Quincey, 1873, pp.109-110).

Addictions are made up of highs and lows which cause the individual to crave more of what is commonly known as 'the buzz'. Thomas De Quincey, a Victorian essayist and academic, published memoirs of his drug addition to 'Laudanum' (which is a combination of alcohol and opium) under the title 'Confessions of an English Opium Eater'.

Interestingly, he divides his work into distinct sections. After giving a history of his early childhood and teenage years, De Quincey discusses his addiction under two titles: 'The Pleasures of Opium' and 'The Pains of Opium' (De Quincey, 1873). This is very indicative and symbolic for us as we study the changes in an individual's personality because we are drawn automatically look at the latter of the two sections and read how his drug addiction cost him and caused him depressive phases which altered his whole behaviour and cognitive thought processes thus by extension modifying his personality temporarily, at first, then permanently. These changes are indicated by his increasing mental and physical problems such as hallucinations, nightmares, reliving of painful memories, insomnia (De Quincey, 1873, p.111) and degeneration of what he calls his 'physical economy' (De Quincey, 1873, p.109).

However, what is also exceptionally interesting is that when De Quincey discusses 'The Pleasures of Opium', we see just as many indicators of personality and behavioural change as he becomes hedonistically addicted to the drug. Some of these changes are seen by De Quincey to be positive since he recalls an event where he gave an acquaintance, called Malay, opium and concludes that since he had not heard of his subsequent death that he 'must have done him the service [he] designed, by giving him one night of respite from the pains of wandering'.

Like the fictional Sherlock Holmes, De Quincey attributes his sharpness of mind to opium and describes it as being able to communicate 'serenity and equipoise to all the faculties, active or passive, and with respect to the temper and moral feelings in general it gives simply that sort of vital warmth which is approved by the judgment' (De Quincey, 1873, p.69). De Quincey then proceeds to demonstrate with a number of autobiographical sketches how opium became his master and he was a slave to it – and importantly for us he describes how his personality became changed greatly as he was 'verging on something very dangerous' (De Quincey, 1873, p.116). In common, day to day words, the 'cravings' for the addictive substance edits an individual's personality as they become more fixated upon its retrieval.

Of course, opium addiction and derivative opiates are just one form of addiction which can modify personality traits. Chemical addictions such as an addiction to stimulants, hallucinogens, sedatives, cocaine, cannabis, alcohol addiction and nicotine addiction, to name a few, can all be tide-turners in the alteration of an individual's personality traits, cognitive functions and behaviour (Miller, 2012, p.220).

Hicks et al. (2012) completed a study which looked at adolescent alcohol dependency and they discovered that personality was 'moderated' by their addiction. By 'moderated' the researchers meant that the addiction the participants had was a leading force in the development of their personalities and changes to their personality profile.

What we must also be careful to note here is that addictions are not just chemical based – for example food addictions or mental illnesses like Anorexia Nervosa and Bulimia Nervosa which can become addictions themselves, an addiction to computer games, addiction to pornography and addictions to gambling. All of the above have the common feature of being able to rapidly modify individual character traits and behaviours certainly lead to temporary changes in personality and then can lead to permanent changes in lifestyle and, by extension, personalities.

McCrady and Epstein (2013) layout some of the possible changes to personality as caused by additions: they note that addicts' personalities can develop and thus they possess the following traits: 'passivity and dependence, an external locus of control, low self-esteem, cognitions that are self-derogatory, depression, anxiety, immaturity, impulsivity [and] anger'. This is important to our study because it demonstrates some of the traits which can alter as a result of personality change and it shows how an individual's personality is key to how they view the world around them, their behaviour, what motivates them and how their personality 'moderates' their decisions.

Chapter Nine

AGE, MATURITY AND PERSONAL GROWTH

Shel Silverstein's 'The Giving Tree'
1964

Once there was a tree and she loved a little boy. And every day the boy would come and he would gather her leaves and make them into crowns and play king of the forest. He would climb up her trunk and swing from her branches and eat apples. And they would play hide-and-go-seek. And when he was tired, he would sleep in her shade. And the boy loved the tree very much. And the tree was happy.

But time went by. And the boy grew older. And the tree was often alone. Then one day the boy came to the tree and the tree said:

"Come, Boy, come and climb up my trunk and swing from my branches and eat apples and play in my shade and be happy."

"I am too big to climb and play" said the boy. "I want to buy things and have fun. I want some money. Can you give me some money?"

"I'm sorry," said the tree, "but I have no money. I have only leaves and apples. Take my apples, Boy, and sell them in city. Then you will have money and you'll be happy."
(Silverstein, 1964, pp.1-17).

'The Giving Tree' is a childhood classic picture book written by Shel Silverstein. The book opens with a happy image of the relationship between a tree and a young boy who enjoy spending time together and playing. With each turn of the page the young boy seems to grow older and by the end of the story the boy is now an old man who has changed beyond recognition. Along the way, the boy revisits the tree over and over. Each time the boy revisits, the tree wants their relationship to return to what it used to be when the boy was small. However, the boy each time gives an excuse and ends up taking part of the tree to use towards his own ends (Silverstein, 1964). There are many interpretations of the meaning of this story, however, for our study, the story does highlight our next area of exploration: the development of personality linked to age and the anthropological idea of 'rites de passage'.

Each time the boy returns to the tree, we see that his focus in life, his emphases have changed. In essence, the person he was has matured and grown – and he has changed in positive ways as well as in, what Silverstein presents, as negative ways. This is indicative of the type of personality development that comes with age: in the beginning, the boy in 'The Giving Tree' just wanted to enjoy himself but as the story continues we see the boy going through many different scenes of life and thus changing into a person we, as readers, do not necessarily like. Silverstein successfully created a simple story that highlights episodic changes in an individual's life that are linked to life milestones – such as needing money of his own, needing a house to live in and marriage.

It can be argued that each of these milestones produce changes in the boy and they affect his outlook on the world. Whether those changes are positive or negative are up for personal interpretation. Each time the boy returns his personality has modified and we see this by the emphases he chooses to focus upon, his level of responsibility, his maturity and his age. Similarly, the Apostle Paul in the 'First Epistle to the Corinthians' states: 'When I was a child, I talked like a child, I thought like a child, I reasoned like a child. When I became a man, I put the ways of childhood behind me' (I Corinthians 13:11). In essence, as the ticking clock is ceaseless in its indication of the passage of time, it is a possibility that personality of an individual is an indicator of time and developmental progress.

This is extremely important to our study of the changes to personality because it is an illustration of how each day of an individual's life there is gradual change and at regular intervals in their life they are able to stop and take stock of how much they have changed and who they developed into because of their experience and the 'rites de passage' they encounter.

Physical life events like puberty, parenting a child, menopause, old age, periods of long term illness will undoubtedly change a person's personality characteristics and their behavioural traits. In addition, we can argue that there are episodic life events of change which will modify an individual's personality because we cannot walk through life events and be mentally unaffected by the experiences we pick up. We learn new skills, we learn from our mistakes, we learn the parameters of social convention and from these things our personality traits are modified or honed. Episodic life events like our first day attending school, transition from primary school to secondary, transition from secondary school to college or university, beginning a career, career changes, retirement, disagreements that we have had with others all affect our personality in different ways.

Haslam et al. (2007) conducted a study looking at the changes in personality as self-reported by undergraduate students. They found a number of interesting features that linked personality changes and stability to age. Firstly, they noted that self-reported emotional stability developed over time until it reached a plateau in late middle age with the trait of agreeableness following a similar pattern. Secondly, they noted that self-reported conscientiousness can be seen increasing rapidly as age progresses until the age of forty-five whereupon it declines. Thirdly, they noted that, from their results, extraversion and openness continued to decline after early adulthood (Haslam et al., 2007, p.1625). This is important because levels of openness to share and levels of openness to change (as well as other personality traits and measurements) might be different depending on an individual's age, past motivations and the 'rites de passage' they have experienced.

Although, in our discussions here, we have established that people's personalities all develop and change with age and progressing through 'rites de passage', we must also acknowledge that it is common sense to recognise that different individuals' personalities will develop at different rates and some people appear to have been modified by their experiences more than others. Therefore, we can confidently assume, personality change can be linked to age as a demographic indicator and age as a partial indicator of maturity.

Mühlig-Versen et al. (2012) followed this idea and attempted to investigate whether it was possible to increase 'levels of openness in later adulthood' and thus examine how correct were the stereotypical patterns of personality evolution linked to age. Their research highlights that although there are noticeable patterns in personality traits and the decrease in levels of openness to new experiences, it was possible to 'facilitate' the change of personality characteristics.

Mühlig-Versen et al. (2012) put it like this: 'the results of this study [is] evidence that age-related declines in openness do not necessarily constitute a natural law of personality development'. Thus, we can say that even though personality is linked to nature, nurture can be an extremely effective force in changing perceptions, behaviour and thus personality characteristics. Consequently, for our study we have established that personality does have a certain 'plasticity' and is able to be modified even when openness to change is not apparent at first. This highlights that discussion around change and metacognitional conversations about attitude and reactions to change might help an individual become better at accepting change or discerning positive change and negative change where in the past they might have been less accepting.

Chapter Ten

PEER INFLUENCE

Friedrich Nietzsche's 'The Dawn of Day'
1881

"A young man can be most surely corrupted when he is taught to value the like-minded more highly than the differently minded."
(Nietzsche, 2007, p.262).

A common phrase that highlights our final area of exploration is that of 'peer pressure'. By peers we mean those who are our friends, our enemies and those in close proximity to us on a regular basis. It is often said that 'he has fallen in with the wrong crowd' or that 'she needs to watch out because they're trouble'. These types of phrases have a profound meaning whether or not we recognise the symbolic meaning of our words. Sayings like these essentially mean that the personality characteristics of those we spend time with and have dealings with can affect our personalities. However, it is important to note here that peer pressure can have perceived positive as well as perceived negative effects.

Goode et al. (2014) completed some social experiments to look at how peer pressure can be used to influence and change behavioural characteristics in positive ways. Their study focused on how undergraduate alcohol consumption is a 'significant public health problem' and thus how a culture has developed which, in some people's opinion, revolves and evolves around excessive drinking as a 'social norm'. One of the experiments first identified leadership within groups of students and which member(s) were prototypical. The researchers then 'primed' members of the group to feel of themselves as role models. Using that member of a social group as an indicator, the researchers we able to see that this decreased the amount of alcohol consumed by the group and by the individual themselves because the individuals sensed a greater responsibility to others around them. This highlights the positive effect peer influence can have on behaviour. One can only assume that, if the experiment was turned on its head and group roles were seen to weaken, we might have seen increased amounts of alcohol consumption. In our discussions so far, we have linked personality developments with behavioural changes and characteristics, thus if we use the experiment conducted by Goode et al. (2014) as an illustration, we can see how the peer pressure might alter personality traits by altering behaviour. If this experiment were continued for an increased amount of time, we might question if it might also help, as a type of training, those with a predisposition to addiction to develop healthier personality traits. This might show that by working with one individual and that they develop as a result of the process, they might have a positive peer influence on other practitioners.

Simons-Morton et al. (2012) completed research into the links between peer influence and 'speeding prevalence among teenage drivers'. The researchers made some interesting discoveries: they found that speeding prevalence was most seen in younger drivers of both genders and in men of all ages - thus highlighting that age and gender have a place in the effects of peer pressure on personality characteristics. However, the most stimulating discovery they made was that peer pressure, speeding and risk taking were all linked. They concluded that 'the only variable that was significantly associated with speeding in multivariate analyses was risky friends' and that 'peer influence is possible the most consistent risk factor for teenage risk behaviour'. This highlights how peer pressure can alter inhibitions and in addition cause behavioural changes in individuals. We might argue that the more these patterns are repeated, the more personality change is likely to occur and that it will influence to what extent personality change happens. In other words, habitual responses are made that repeat and repeat and thus alter personality traits.

Similar types of studies have been conducted to predict smoking habits of adolescents (Perrine and Aloise-Young, 2004) and also in 'willingness to engage in antisocial activity' (Steinberg & Monahan, 2007). In both of these studies, and countless more, the same patterns appear indicating the possibility for the modification of personality traits which can sometimes be perceived in positive ways and sometimes in negative ways. In essence, we become like those who we spend time with whether that is a spouse, partner, friend, colleague.

Nietzsche notes, in his collection of philosophical ideas called 'The Dawn of Day', that there is a danger when people conform to peer pressure and the ideals and patterns of behaviour of like-minded people rather than considering the wider picture and the opinions of others (Nietzsche, 2007, p.262). In essence, what Nietzsche is suggesting that we should learn to consider more and more opinions rather than blindly follow the herd. This highlights and illustrates for us two polar types of development. However, both of these developments demonstrate that our lives, perspectives and thus our personalities can be modified by those around us. We can either, as Nietzsche states, align our thinking at times with those who are like-minded and thus we become modified by in a very insular way: our personalities can be modified even if only minutely to be more similar to those who we consider like-minded and thus we might argue a group mentality of correlating opinions and personalities is slowly being created. In other words, a blinkered development.

We can argue that, at times, we are influenced by others opinions not just those who are in our peer groups or those who are our spouses or partners. This type of development in personality, behaviour or cognition can produce two results: external peer pressure can mean that we concur with others who we do not consider to be in our peer group or we can react against their opinions and think or do the opposite. An illustration of this could be appearance: walking around any town or shopping centre it is possible to see so many different types of clothing choices, tattoos, piercings etc. There are those who conform to the contemporary styles and fashion. There are those who specifically choose to create alternative styles thus reacting against the common 'zeitgeist' of fashion and often being different in order to achieve a reaction from peers or from others members of their communities. Then there are those who are not necessarily pioneers of fashion but they are followers and conformers of the reactionary alternative styles modelled by others. Hunt (2013) note that these individuals are 'enabled' by the influence of others to develop. Thus, we can see that peer pressure can work so that some individuals develop and conform to be more like their peers and thus this can often be an indicator of personality changes. On the other hand, there are those who react against peer pressure – and therefore they are attempting to be different which can itself often be an indicator of personality change. Either way these types of changes to personality characteristics, as highlighted by Nietzsche, can either introduced into our personality or if we already possessed these characteristics they can be developed and strengthened. It is important to note here that these types of changes can be conscious decisions or subconscious decisions which then in turn modify our personality.

During the course of this chapter we have looked at how others influence our personality and have established how behaviour influence is a key factor in the development of personality traits. Now that we have studied nine different categories of reasons behind personality change, we need to look at all the categories and how they fit together.

Chapter Eleven

CONCLUSION

Over the course of this book, we have established that personality is changeable and that change can come in various different guises. We have seen how some changes can be long developing whilst others are almost instant reactionary changes to stimuli.

In addition, we have demonstrated how changes might be temporary, long lasting or even permanent. However, what our study of the research literature has shown is that personality changes are not necessarily incidents; rather every person is constantly going through the process of change and it is the direction, severity and speed of the changes which are different. Some changes to personality can be perceived by the individual, or by others, as desirable progressions and thus are seen as positive modifications to a person's traits, behaviour and cognitive functions. On the other hand, other personality changes can be seen as undesirable developments and thus are negative developments causing alterations and adjustments to an individual's psyche, thought process, motivations and actions.

Over the course of nine chapters, we have established a set of categories which spell out a number of significant reasons behind personality change and looked at the nuances of each category.

i.   Using George Bernard Shaw's 'Pygmalion' we delved into the possibilities that individuals could consciously, or unconsciously, be trained or coached to possess different personality characteristics.

ii.   We have established how religious conversion or even conversion from a religion to agnosticism or atheism can cause sudden character transformation or long-developing trait changes. We discussed the idea of a revelation or epiphany as a result of personality assessment.

iii.   Using Sylvia Plath as an illustrative case study, we have examined how mental illnesses such as bipolar disorder can produce sets of personality characteristics that can oscillate in an individual's life. Additionally, we observed how these changes to an individual's personality can also produce changes in the personalities of those around them.

iv.   As stimulus for discussing trauma's effect on an individual's personality, we examined Virginia Woolf's character, Septimus, and his Post-Traumatic Stress Disorder (PTSD). We appreciated that trauma's effect on the personality of an individual can be physical or emotional, or a mixture of the both, and that trauma can have a delayed effect on the personality. We discussed how trauma such as workplace bullying can affect personality.

v.   During our discussion of changes in political allegiances and moral perspective amendments, we explored how political changes that cause personality modification can be conscious cognitive alterations or can be subliminal. We investigated two examples of indoctrination and its effects on the individual and on the relative mass populations.

vi.   Making use of Samantha Harvey's novel, 'The Wilderness', we examined how memory degeneration and frontotemporal lobar deterioration can cause significant personality changes to a point where the individual is almost unrecognisable to others and to themselves.

vii.   Thomas De Quincey's memoirs launched us into our discussion of addiction as a catalyst for personality change. We examined how perceived changes to personality can begin in a way in which the addict comprehends as positive changes before they become seen as negative. Addiction often causes profound changes to an individual's personality which then 'moderate' behaviour and cognitive functionality.

viii.   Following this we inspected the effects of aging on the personality and discussed how 'rites de passage' can modify and hone our personalities. Using a variety of previous studies, we established that certain personality characteristics are likely at specific stages of life.

ix.   Finally, we examined how peer influence can effectively modify personality characteristics and behaviour in both positive and negative ways in both the short term and long term.

These discussions have proved that personality has a certain plasticity regardless of age, gender, predisposition and personal experience. They have also established that there is an undeniable link between personality characteristics, behaviour and cognitive function that was set out by our examination into the definitions of personality. The research demonstrates how visible and audible behaviour (that is actions taken by an individual) and invisible cognitive function (that is beliefs and thoughts, understanding, motivations and stream of consciousness) are manifestations of personality traits that are at the core of an individual (which we might call, in Freudian terms, the psyche). Thus, if we observe changes in these areas, it is likely that personality traits have altered because new 'specific' and 'habitual responses' will have begun manifesting themselves.

In addition, we have seen how the nine categories as outlined in our discussions of the research literature are extremely significant factors in personality change. However, we have seen how they overlap and it is likely that when we observe personality changes it is because of a combination of these factors.

At this point, we must also note that it is possible that an individual will experience personality changes caused by these reasons at multiple points in their lives. For instance, trauma that causes personality change in childhood can lead to substance abuse in teenage years (which itself causes personality modification) and thus this can lead mental illness in early adulthood (which then in turn, again, causes alteration of personality characteristics). This string of developments highlights that the reasons for personality change we have discussed can be described as chain reactionary and produce a downward spiralling effect. Similarly, the chain reaction can also cause an upward spiral. For instance, training and coaching to introduce or strengthen perceived, desirable personality traits can then lead to positive peer pressure (which itself causes further modification) and then a more stable mental health.

Akin to this type of upward spiral, an individual could experience religious conversion and thus their political and moral allegiances are modified (which itself causes additional alteration to the personality) which can then lead to positive peer influence and personal maturity.

In conclusion, personality changes and modifications are complex. Over the course of this concise text, we have attempted to scope out the underlying foundational reasons behind personality change in an accessible way so that the literary illustrations help to ground abstract academic theory in concrete examples.

Academic References

BOOKS AND JOURNAL ARTICLES

Altieri, S., Singh, Y., Sibille, E. & Andrews, A. (2013) 'Serotonergic Pathways in Depression', in Lopez-Munoz, F. & Alamo, C. (eds.) *Neurobiology of Depression*. Florida: Taylor & Francis Group. pp.143-159.

Aziz, R. (1990) *C. G. Jung's Psychology of Religion and Synchronicity*. New York: State University of New York Press.

Barnes, A. (2007) *Seeing through Self-Deception*. Cambridge: Cambridge University Press.

Bernard Shaw, B. (2000) *Pygmalion: A Romance in Five Acts*. London: Penguin.

Bonhoeffer, D. (2015) *The Cost of Discipleship*. London: SCM Press.

Briggs-Myers, I. & Myers, P. (2010) *Gifts Differing: Understanding Personality Type*. California: CPP, Inc.

Broughton, D. & Ten Napel, H. (2000) *Religion and Mass Electoral Behaviour in Europe*. London: Routledge.

Brunas-Wagstaff, J. (1998) *Personality: A Cognitive Approach*. London: Routledge.

Caligor, E., Kernberg, O. & Clarkin, J. (2007) *Handbook of Dynamic Psychotherapy for Higher Level Personality Pathology*. Arlington: American Psychiatric Publishing.

Carducci, B. (2009) *The Psychology of Personality: Viewpoints, Research and Applications.* Chichester: John Wiley & Sons.

Carstensen, L., Mikels, J. & Mather, M. (2011) 'Aging and the Intersection of Cognition, Motivation and Emotion', in Birren, J. & Schaie, K. (eds.) *Handbook of the Psychology of Aging.* California: Academic Press. pp.343-356.

Cervone, D. & Shoda, Y. (1999) *The Coherence of Personality: Social-cognitive Bases of Consistency, Variability, and Organization.* New York: Guilford Press.

Cervone, D. & Pervin, L. (2015) *Personality: Theory and Research.* New York: John Wiley and Sons.

Chu, J. (1998) Rebuilding Shattered Lives: The Responsible Treatment of Complex Post-Traumatic and Dissociative Disorders. Oxford: John Wiley & Sons Ltd.

Clark, D., Ehlers, A., McManus, F., Hackmann, A., Fennell, M., Campbell, H. & Louis, B. (2003) 'Cognitive therapy versus fluoxetine in generalized social phobia: A randomized placebo-controlled trial', *Journal of Consulting and Clinical Psychology*, 71(1). pp.1058-1067.

Cole, A. (2016) *Does body language communicate personality? Observable behavioural patterns of Berens Interactions Styles.* Germany: Grin Verlag.

Coon, D. & Mitterer, J. (2008) *Introduction to Psychology: Gateways to Mind and Behaviour.* Belmont: Cengage Learning.

Cooper, C. (2010) *Individual Differences and Personality.* Abingdon: Routledge.

Crozier, W. (2013) *Individual Learners: Personality Differences in Education.* Abingdon: Routledge.

Cull, N., Holbrook, D. & Welch, D. (2003) *Propaganda and Mass Persuasion.* California: ABC-CLIO.

Daly, R. & Sand. E. (2012) *Psychological Treatment of Mental Illness: Research Strategies and Design*. Heidelbeeg: Springer-Verlag.

De Berg, H. (2004) *Freud's Theory and It's Use in Literary and Cultural Studies: An Introduction*. New York: Camden House.

De Quincey, T. (1873) *Confessions of an English Opium Eater*. Boston: James R. Osgood and Company.

Derksen, J., Maffei, C. & Groen, H. (1999) *Treatment of Personality Disorders*. New York: Kluwer Academic.

De Wit, H. (2005) 'Relationships Between Personality and Acute Subjective Responses to Stimulant Drugs', in Earleywine, M. (ed.) *Mind-Altering Drugs: The Science of Subjective Experience*. Oxford: Oxford University Press. pp. 258-274.

Dittmann, M. (2002) 'Cults of Hatred', in *Monitor*, 33(10). p.30.

Dolan-Sewell, R., Krueger, R. & Shea, M. (2001) 'Co-Occurrence with Syndrome Disorders', in Livesley, W. (eds.) *Handbook of Personality Disorders: Theory, Research and Treatment*. New York: Guilford Press. pp.84-107.

Engler, B. (2013) *Personality Theories*. California: Cengage Learning.

Eysenck, H. (1950) *Dimensions of Personality*. New Brunswick: Transaction Publishers.

Farrell, D. (2010) *Examples and Principles of Psychology in the Bible*. Enumclaw: Redemption Press.

Fisher, S. & Van Der Kolk, B. (2014) *Neurofeedback in the Treatment of Developmental Trauma: Calming the Fear-Driven Brain*. New York: W.W. Norton & Company.

Fleminger, S. (2010) 'Head Injury', in David, A., Fleminger, S., Kopelman, M., Lovestone, S., Folstein, M. & Mellers, J. (eds.) *Lishman's*

Organic Psychiatry: A Textbook of Neuropsychiatry. Oxford: John Wiley & Sons Ltd. pp.167-280.

Ford, M. (2010) *Body Language: and Behavioral Profiling*. Bloomington: Author House.

Freud, S. (2016) *Das Ich und Das Es*. Agile: FV Éditions.

Freeth, R. (2007) *Humanising Psychiatry and Mental Health Care: The Challenge of the Person-centred Approach*. Abingdon: Radcliffe Publishing.

Galen, C. 1968. *Galen on the Usefulness of the Parts of the Body*. New York: Cornell University Press.

Gallucci, G. 2001. *Plato and Freud: Statesmen of the Soul*. Indiana: Xlibris Corporation.

Geiger, E., Kelley, M. & Nation, P. (2012) *Transformational Discipleship: How People Really Grow*. Nashville, Tennessee: B&H Publishing Group.

Gillon, E. (2007) *Person-Centred Counselling Psychology: An Introduction*. London: Sage Publications.

Goode, C., Balzarini, R. & Smith, H. (2014) 'Positive Peer Pressure: Priming Member Prototypicality Can Decrease Undergraduate Drinking', in *Journal of Applied Social Psychology,* 44(1). pp.567-578.

Gross, R. (2015) *Psychology: The Science of Mind and Behaviour*. London: Hodder and Stoughton.

Hampson, S. (2000) *Advances in Personality Psychology*. Hove: Psychology Press.

Harvey, S. (2010) *The Wilderness*. London: Random House.

Haslam, N., Bastian, B., Fox, C. & Whelan, J. (2007) 'Beliefs about Personality Change and Continuity', in *Personality and Individual Differences*, 42(1). pp.1621-1631.

Herf, J. (2014) 'Narrative and Mendacity: Anti-Semitic Propaganda in Nazi Germany', in Auerbach, J. & Castronovo, R. (eds.) *The Oxford Handbook of Propaganda Studies*. New York: Oxford University Press. pp.91-108.

Hicks, B., Durbin, C., Blonigen, D., Iacono, W. & McGue, M. (2011) 'Relationship between personality change and the onset and course of alcohol dependence in young adulthood', in *Addiction*, 107(1). pp.540-548.

Hiemer, E. (1938) *Der Giftpliz*. Berlin: Julius Streicher.

Hinshaw, S. (2007) *Breaking the Silence: Mental Health Professionals Disclose Their Personal and Family Experiences of Mental Illness*. California: Oxford University Press.

Hirst, P. (2010) 'From Revelation and Faith to Reason and Agnosticism', in Caws, P. & Jones, S. (eds.) *Religions Upbringing and the Costs of Freedom: Personal and Philosophical Essays*. Pennsylvania: Pennsylvania State University. pp.155-175.

Hudson, N. & Fraley, R. (2015) 'Personality Trait Change: Can People Choose to Change Their Personality Traits?', in *Journal of Personality and Social Psychology*, 109(3). pp.490-507.

Hunt, N. (2013) 'Young People and Illicit Drug Use', in Aggleton, P. & Ball, A. *Sex, Drugs and Young People: International Perspectives*. Abingdon: Routledge. pp.84-100.

James, W. (1890) *Principles of Psychology*. New York: Holt.

Jung, C. (1926) *Psychological Types or the Psychology of Individuation*. London: Kegan Paul, Trench, Trübner & Company.

Kalat, J. (2010) *Introduction to Psychology*. California: Cengage Learning.

Kelly, N., Rees, B. & Shuter, P. (2003) *Medicine through Time*. Oxford, Heinemann.

Kline, P. (2013) *Personality: The Psychometric View*. Hove: Routledge.

Lall, M. & Sharma, S. (2012) *Personal Growth and Training and Development*. New Delhi: Excel Books.

Lee, S. (2005) *Hitler and Nazi Germany*. London: Routledge.

Lucia, C. (2013) 'Educating Rita and the Pygmalion Effect: Gender, Class and Adaptation Anxiety', in Parmer, R. & Bray, W. (eds.) *Modern British Drama on Screen*. Cambridge: Cambridge University Press. pp.192-215.

Magison, J., Roberts, B., Collado-Rodriguez, A. & Lejuez, C. (2014) 'Theory-Driven Intervention for Changing Personality: Expectancy Value Theory, Behavioral Activation, and Conscientiousness', in *Developmental Psychology*, 50(5). pp.1442-1450.

Mahoney, C., Rohrer, J., Omar, R., Rossor, M. & Warren, J. (2011) 'Neuroanatomical profiles of personality change in frontotemporal lobar degeneration', in *The British Journal of Psychiatry*, 198(1). pp.365-372.

Matthews, G., Deary, I. & Whiteman, M. (2009) *Personality Traits*. Cambridge: Cambridge University Press.

McCrady, B. & Epstein, E. (2013) *Addictions: A Comprehensive Guidebook*. New York: Oxford University Press.

Meier, S. (2010) *An Investigation into the Relationship Between Instructional Leadership Processes and Personality*. New York: University of Rochester Press.

Mendy, G. (2013) *Augustine's Spirit-Soul Analogy and its Implication for Communion Ecclesiology.* Indiana: Xlibris.

Miller, N. (2012) *The Pharmacology of Alcohol and Drugs of Abuse and Addiction.* New York: Springer-Verlag.

Mondak, J. (2010) *Personality and the Foundations of Political Behavior.* Cambridge: Cambridge University Press.

Mühlig-Versen, A., Bowen, C. & Staudinger, U. (2012) 'Personality Plasticity in Later Adulthood: Contextual and Personal Resources Are Needed to Increase Openness to New Experiences', in *Psychology and Aging,* 27(4). pp.855-866.

Newton, J. (1831) *The Works of the Rev. John Newton: Volume 1.* Philadelphia: Uriah Hunt.

Nietzsche, F. (2007) *The Dawn of Day.* Mineola: Dover Publications Inc.

Paloutzian, R., Richardson, J. & Rambo, L. (1999) 'Religious Change and Personality Change', *Journal of Personality,* 67(6). pp.1047-1079.

Parkin, A. (2013) *Memory and Amnesia: An Introduction.* Oxford: Blackwell Publishers Ltd.

Pavlov, I. (1902) *The Work of the Digestive Glands.* London: Griffin.

Perrine, N. & Aloise-Young, P. (2004) 'The Role of Self-Monitoring in Adolescents' Susceptibility to Passive Peer Pressure', in *Personality and Individual Differences,* 37(1). pp.1701-1716.

Plath, S. (2005) *The Bell Jar.* London: Faber and Faber Limited.

Plath, S. (2000) *The Unabridged Journals of Sylvia Plath, 1950-1962.* New York: Anchor Books.

Pocnet, C., Rossier, J., Antonietti, J. & Von Gunten, A. (2013) 'Personality features and cognitive level in patients at an early stage of Alzheimer's disease', in *Personality and Individual Differences*, 54(1). pp.174-179.

Progoff, I. (2013) *Jung's Psychology and its Social Meaning: An Introductory Statement of C. G. Jung's Psychological Theories and a First Interpretation of their Significance for the Social Sciences*. New York: Routledge.

Quenk, N. (2009) *Essentials of Myers-Briggs Type Indicator Assessment*. Oxford: John Wiley & Sons.

Rennison, N. (2015) *Freud and Psychoanalysis*. London: Oldcastle Books.

Roberts, B. & Hudson, N. (2014) 'Goals to Change Personality Traits: Concurrent Links Between Personality Traits, Daily Behaviour and Goals to Change Oneself', in *Journal of Research in Personality*, 53(1). pp.68-83.

Rogers, C. (1959). 'A Theory of Therapy, Personality, and Interpersonal Relationships, as Developed in the Client-Centered Framework', in Koch, S. (ed.) *Psychology: A Study of a Science*. New York: McGraw-Hill. pp.184-246.

Sandler, J. (1997) *Freud's Models of the Mind: An Introduction*. London: Karnac Books.

Schacter, D., Gilbert, D. Wegner, D. & Hood, B. (2011) *Psychology*. Basingstoke: Palgrave Macmillan.

Sharf, W. (2012) *Theories of Psychotherapy & Counselling: Concepts and Cases*. Belmont: Brooks and Cole.

Silverman, H. & Ihde, D. 1985. *Hermeneutics and Deconstruction*. New York: University of New York Press.

Silverstein, S. (1964) *The Giving Tree*. New York: HarperCollins.

Simons-Morton, B., Ouimet, M., Chen, R., Klauer, S., Lee, S., Wang, J. & Dingus, T. (2012) 'Peer Influence Predicts Speeding Prevalence Among Teenage Drivers', in *Journal of Safety Research,* 43(1). pp.397-403.

Smith, B. (2010) *The Key of Green: Passion and Perception in Renaissance Culture.* Chicago: University of Chicago Press.

Spar, J. & La Rue, A. (2007) *Clinical Manual of Geriatric Psychiatry.* Arlington: American Psychiatric Publishing, Inc.

Steinberg, L. & Monahan, K. (2007) 'Age Differences in Resistance to Peer Influence', in *Developmental Psychology,* 43(6). pp.1531-1543.

Stringer, S., Hurn, J. & Husain, M. (2015) *Psychiatry: Breaking the Ice.* Oxford: John Wiley & Sons Ltd.

Strong, J. (2009) *Strong's Exhaustive Concordance to the Bible.* Massachusetts: Hendrickson Publishers.

Talassi, E., Guerreschi, M., Feriani, M., Fedi, V., Bianchetti, A. & Trabucchi, M. (2007) 'Effectiveness of a Cognitive Rehabilitation Program in Mild Dementia (MD) and Mild Cognitive Impairment (MCI): A Case Control Study', in *Archives of Gerontology and Geriatrics,* 44(1), pp.391-399.

Taylor, K. (2006) *Brainwashing: The Science of Thought Control.* Oxford: Oxford University Press.

Terraciano, A., Iancno, D., O'Brien, R., Troncoso, J., An, Y., Sutin, A. & Resnick, S. (2013) 'Personality and Resilience to Alzheimer's Disease Neuropathology: A Prospective Autopsy Study', in *Neurobiology of Aging,* 34(1), pp.1045-1050.

Tickle, J., Heatherton, T. & Wittenberg, L. (2001) 'Can Personality Change?', in Livesley, W. (ed.) *Handbook of Personality Disorders: Theory, Research and Treatment.* New York: Guilford Press. pp.243-258.

Vidal, F. (2011) *The Sciences of the Soul: The Early Modern Origins of Psychology*. London: University of Chicago Press.

Wagner, E. (2001) *Essays on Plato's Psychology*. Maryland: Lexington Books.

Wilkins, P. (2016) *Person-Centred Therapy*. London: Routledge.

Wolitzky, D. (2006) 'Psychodynamic Theories', in Thomas, J. & Segal, D. (eds.) *Comprehensive Handbook of Personality and Psychopathology, Personality and Everyday Functioning*. New Jersey: John Wiley & Sons.

Woolf, V. (2013) *Mrs. Dalloway*. London: Harper Press.

FILMS

Der Ewige Jude (1940) Directed by Fritz Hippler [Film]. Germany: Deutsche Film Gesellschaft.

SACRED TEXTS

Acts 9:1-6, Holy Bible, New International Version.

Acts 9:19b-22, Holy Bible, New International Version.

I Corinthians 13:11, Holy Bible, New International Version.